The Physician's Guide to Buying a House

Goldie Winge, MD

HOUSING 911
Published by Purposely Created Publishing Group™
Copyright © 2018 Goldie Winge

All rights reserved.

No part of this book may be reproduced, distributed or transmitted in any form by any means, graphic, electronic, or mechanical, including photocopy, recording, taping, or by any information storage or retrieval system, without permission in writing from the publisher, except in the case of reprints in the context of reviews, quotes, or references.

This book is for information and educational purposes only and should not be misconstrued as official financial advice. Please consult with your financial advisor.

Printed in the United States of America
ISBN: 978-1-948400-49-7

Special discounts are available on bulk quantity purchases by book clubs, associations and special interest groups. For details email:
sales@publishyourgift.com
or call (888) 949-6228.

For information logon to:
www.PublishYourGift.com

DEDICATION

This book is dedicated to people in the medical profession who work hard every day to provide safe and compassionate care. Your hard work is appreciated, and you deserve to live in the house of your dreams. After going through an arduous and long escrow process myself, I promised that I would help others avoid the many pitfalls and heartbreaks I faced. My mission is to educate doctors and professionals on how to find, fix, and finance the house of their dreams!

TABLE OF CONTENTS

Introduction 1

CHAPTER 1:
Should I Buy a House? 3

CHAPTER 2:
Positioning Yourself to Buy 7

CHAPTER 3:
Location, Location, Location 13

CHAPTER 4:
The Right Agent Means the Right House 17

CHAPTER 5:
Finding the Right House Is Easier than Ever ... 21

CHAPTER 6:
Financing Your Home 25

CHAPTER 7:
Putting In an Offer 29

CHAPTER 8:
Offer Accepted! Now What? 33

CHAPTER 9:
Escrow 37

CHAPTER 10:
The Underwriting Process 41

CHAPTER 11:
Closing the Deal 45

Acknowledgments 49

About the Author 53

INTRODUCTION

Over the past several years, the real estate market has been in full recovery mode. While this has been good news for many homeowners, it has made it much more challenging for prospective homeowners to buy an affordable house. High- cost-of-living areas such as a Los Angeles, California seem daunting. That's where I come in. This book is a step-by-step guide to affording and buying the house of your dreams. You deserve it!

CHAPTER 1

SHOULD I BUY A HOUSE?

Buying a house is a big decision. In fact, a house will most likely be the biggest purchase you will make in your lifetime. It is worthwhile to sit down with your tax or financial advisor and crunch the numbers.

Does it make more sense to buy or rent? This is an important question that must be carefully considered. Once you know that you want to stay in the same location for the next five to seven years, you should consider buying a house. As a doctor, you've spent some of the best years of your life in medical school, and it feels like it's time to finally catch up to your non-medical friends. Buying a house should not be based on emotions. It should be based on what makes sense financially. If you still aren't sure whether you should rent or buy, there are plenty of rent vs. buy calculators online. Bankrate has one: http://www.bankrate.com/calculators/mortgages/rent-or-buy-home.aspx

Here's one from realtor.com: http://www.realtor.com/mortgage/tools/rent-or-buy-calculator/

The great thing about buying a house is that it's all yours. You want to paint it, change the carpet, put in hardwood floors, it's your call. Buying a house is a great way to build wealth. Over time, most homes will appreciate in value. Whereas rent will continue to go up over the years, your mortgage only goes up slightly over time, assuming you have a fixed interest rate. The principal and interest will stay the same, but the home insurance and taxes will only increase a small amount each year.

Buying a house has many rewards. It also comes with a lot of responsibilities. You will need to quickly get out of the renter mentality. The buck stops with you. No more putting in work orders and then forgetting about it. A leaky faucet means either fixing it yourself or calling a plumber, coordinating a time, and paying for their services.

The tax benefits of a house will change depending on the tax laws. In general, you are able to write off part of the interest you pay on your mortgage and part of your property tax. You are also able to write off part of your closing costs. Again, tax laws can change year to year. I recommend getting your taxes done by a professional when you buy a house.

The best time to buy a house depends on the individual. As a general rule, you should buy a house if you plan on living in it for at least five to seven years. That means that buying a house in residency and fellowship doesn't make sense unless you know for sure that you won't be moving. I suggest that even as a new attending, you should wait at least six months to a year to buy a house after finding a job. That allows you to really know if you like your new job and the city you are in.

CHAPTER 2

POSITIONING YOURSELF TO BUY

Once you have decided to buy a house, it becomes a process. The best way to set yourself up to buy a house is to prepare in advance. That means becoming the best candidate possible. The first thing you should do is start saving for a down payment. Traditionally, a down payment for a house is 20 percent of the purchase price. Putting 20 percent down is ideal because you will get the best mortgage interest rate and avoid paying private mortgage insurance (PMI). However, there are plenty of loan products that allow you to place less than 20 percent down. These types of loan products may or may not require PMI. The good news is that if you are paying PMI, once your house gains 20 percent equity, you may be able to stop paying PMI.

The next step to position yourself as a good buyer is to have excellent credit. Being a physician is not the only criterion you need to qualify for a physician loan. There are minimum credit score requirements too. The minimum credit score varies by loan program, but you would obviously want to have the best score possible, as it also affects the interest rate you will be given.

The first thing you need to do is get your credit report. You can get a copy of your report annually without cost. The website is: www.annualcreditreport.com. The three major credit bureaus are TransUnion, Equifax, and Experian. Your credit score basically indicates your credit worthiness, or how likely you are to pay your debt. Each bureau gives you multiple FICO scores. The FICO score used to determine your eligibility for a home loan is much stricter than the ones used for getting a cell phone or buying a car. It's also important to note that banks often use your median score, or middle score, to determine whether or not you meet the minimum criteria for a home loan.

Go over your entire credit report, paying special attention to errors or misinformation. If there are any errors on your credit report, you need to contact each bureau individually and fix it. This can take time, so it is very important to start this process at least six months before you plan on buying a house. You will hardly ever need to use a service to "fix your credit." If you have an overdue bill, pay it. Then you can ask the creditor to remove their negative mark off your credit. Oftentimes they are willing to do it if you are up to date on your balance and ask nicely. This is especially true for utility companies. Once the creditor removes that negative mark from your credit, your score will increase. Several factors influence your credit score, such as paying bills on time, available credit on your credit accounts, and how long you have had credit. Credit scores range from 300-850. Poor credit is generally less than 650, fair is 650-699, good is 700-739, very good is 740-799, and excellent is greater than 800.

Another important thing to do before buying a house is to live on a strict budget. A budget allows you to be consistent every month with your expenses and savings. When you are getting approved for a home loan, the bank will monitor every purchase you make and compare it to your past habits. This is the loan underwriting process. During that process, they will constantly ask you about any unusual spending. If you deviate from your past spending habits, it will raise a red flag. That is the last thing you want to do while awaiting approval for a home loan. During the six months to one year before buying a house, try not to make any large purchases, such as cars or major appliances. You can buy that new car or state-of-the-art washer and dryer after you buy your house. Also, try to avoid opening new lines of credits such as credit cards. These create inquiries on your credit and can actually lower your credit score if you get enough of them.

Paying your bills on time should go without saying. However, doctors lead busy lives. It can be easy to forget when a bill is due. The best way to avoid late payments and bad credit is to pay your bills on time. This helps to show the bank that you are a consistent person. They like to loan money to consistent and reliable people. A great way to avoid paying your bills late is to use automatic payments. If you don't want to do that, I suggest you pay your bills the same time every month. That way you won't forget.

CHAPTER 3

LOCATION, LOCATION, LOCATION

Now that you have decided to buy a house, have excellent credit, and live on a budget, it's important for you to decide on a location. What makes a good location? It depends on the individual. Things to consider include work commute time, the safety of the neighborhood, the school district, accessibility to freeways, the aesthetics of the neighborhood, and accessibility to parks, playgrounds, and libraries.

The Internet has valuable information about neighborhoods, such as crime statistics, annual household incomes, zoning, types of businesses nearby, and walkability scores. For example, the *Los Angeles Times* has a website with this type of information. There are also blogs online that have information on different neighborhoods and communities. An important consideration is the neighborhood school. There is a 1-10 ranking score of schools. Good schools increase property value and desirability. They also allow you to save money on tuition. A growing trend in Los Angeles public schools is to ask for donations from parents to help out with school activities and programs. These donations are still way less expensive than private schools in Los Angeles, which can range from $500 to thousands of dollars per month.

You can learn valuable information about a neighborhood by driving around it in the afternoon, night, and early morning and on the weekend. I also suggest walking around the neighborhood. This helps you get a feel for what it is like to interact with the residents. Another way to get to know the neighborhood is to go to open houses. While you are at the open house, you will meet agents who often have other properties coming up on the market that may not have been listed on the Multiple Listing Service (MLS). The MLS is a database of houses that are for sale. These can give you a heads up on homes to come. This is why it is imperative that you have a clear picture of what kind of house you want.

Once you have decided on the location where you want to live, I highly suggest getting a real estate agent who is very familiar with that particular neighborhood. There are nuances to every neighborhood, and being one block east or west can affect your home value and your happiness with the location. What's the most important thing to consider in real estate? Location, location, location. You can change all sorts of things about a house: the landscaping, paint, roof, floors. But you can't change the location. It's better to buy a smaller or older house in a nice neighborhood than to get the most elaborate house in an undesirable neighborhood.

When deciding on a location, you should be aware of the businesses, schools, and parks nearby. For example, if there is a railroad nearby, make sure that you are around when the train actually passes by. Don't take other people's word on how loud something is. Living near a school may sound convenient, but oftentimes parents are in a rush to drop off or pick up their children. That leads to traffic congestion, double parking, blocked driveways, and lots of noise from children. Homes that are in very close proximity to schools and parks tend to be less desirable and have lower values.

CHAPTER 4

THE RIGHT AGENT MEANS THE RIGHT HOUSE

Your real estate agent should not only represent you, but should also be your advocate and trusted advisor. Your real estate agent will be handling all the paperwork involved with the escrow process and be the middleman during that process. There are some websites that say you don't need an agent or that you should use the seller's agent. I do not recommend that for a first-time homebuyer. Real estate agents navigate the housing market for a living and should be able to advise you on homes to see, how much you should offer on the house, and the strategy you should use for making that offer. As a buyer, you are not the one who will directly pay your agent. The seller will be paying both their agent and your agent's commission. Standard commission on a house is 6 percent. The commission is typically split 50/50 between the buyer and seller's agent. Pick a reliable real estate agent who consistently looks for homes for you, has experience and influence, and is familiar with the area in which you want to buy.

You may be asking yourself, "Where am I going to find this wonderful agent?" The best way is word of mouth. Ask your homeowner friends if they were happy with their agent. If the answer is yes, then ask for that agent's number. Contact the agent and tell him or her what you are looking for. Ask if he or she is an expert in the particular location you are looking for. If he/she is not, ask for a recommended colleague. As a physician, you are knowledgeable about medicine in general, but you are likely a specialist in one or two things. You ask for a consult when you need specific expertise on a medical problem. Do the same for real estate.

If you don't know a good agent, then go to open houses. Let me tell you a secret: the open house is not primarily for people to look at houses. It is also for agents to get new customers. One of the first questions an agent at an open house asks is "Are you working with an agent?" If not, they will try to get your business. Having gone to countless open houses, I have seen this time and time again. In fact, the agent who is at the open house is often not even the listing agent. Why is that? The listing agent is closing other deals. Homes can easily be shown privately. That's the purpose of a lock box. The lock box contains the key to the house and is secured by a code. Your agent can easily arrange a private showing for you.

Once you have found a great real estate agent, the next step is to decide on your must-haves and negotiables. I would start with location. Next, I would decide on a single-family home, condo, or townhouse. Oftentimes townhomes and condos have an HOA (Home Owner Association). These governing bodies decide on which renovations are done and are responsible for the outside of your home and communal structures, such as elevators and community rooms. They charge a monthly fee. For every $400 you pay in HOA monthly fees, you can buy $100,000 more in a house. In other words, the total mortgage payment on a $500,000 single-family home is approximately the same as a $400,000 condo with a $400 a month HOA.

CHAPTER 5

FINDING THE RIGHT HOUSE IS EASIER THAN EVER

Finding the right house is easier than ever with the Internet and phone apps such as Redfin, Zillow, and realtor.com. These sites utilize the MLS to give up-to-date information on homes for sale, such as square footage, number of bedrooms and bathrooms, and lot sizes. Sites such as Redfin and Zillow also give estimates on home values, which can be very helpful in deciding if a house is potentially a good deal. These sites may also have information on how much the home was last sold for. Your real estate agent will have full access to the MLS, which will have a treasure trove of information, such as how much is still owed on the house and if it's going to be a standard sale. Once you have identified a house you like, you should see it as quickly as possible. In hot markets like Los Angeles, San Francisco, and New York, appropriately priced homes go very quickly due to low inventory.

A great way to find a house is through open houses. Open houses tend to be on Saturdays and Sundays between noon and 5pm. The listing agent may not be there, but there may be another agent from their company who is looking for new clients. Open houses are also a low-pressure way to inspect a house you are interested in.

Most people will go to an open house and just look. A smart buyer will inspect as much as they can and not wait until being in escrow. You should be opening and closing doors, turning on faucets, looking at the overall condition of the house, and evaluating the drainage systems outside, to name a few tasks. This, of course, does not replace a detailed home inspection. This does, however, give you valuable information without having to enter into escrow and then be disappointed. I have noticed major structural and roofing issues just from observations made at an open house.

The time of the year affects the inventory of houses. Summer has the highest inventory of houses. As you can imagine, people prefer to move during the summer. The school year has ended and many people are on vacation. This is an ideal time to move. The winter has the lowest inventory. Also, there are many holidays during the fall and winter. This can mean delays in processing paperwork due to holidays and vacation. Keep that in mind if you enter into escrow near the end of the calendar year.

Another great way to find a house is word of mouth. Real estate agents may have pocket listings. These are homes for sale that have not been put on the market. The sellers want to sell their house, but only a select few know about it. Having a well-connected and experienced real estate agent can put you in the know.

Friends and family can also connect you to a great house. If you are in the market for a house, let your friends and family know right away. They may be able to get you connected to your dream house. One of my medical school classmates told me he was interested in moving to my neighborhood. He had been waiting for the perfect house to go on the market for over a year! As luck would have it, I saw an open house sign. I went out of curiosity, saw the house, and loved it. I found out it wasn't listed on the MLS yet because they were hoping for a neighbor to refer it to a friend. That made me immediately think of my classmate. I called him right away, and he came over to see the house. He and his wife ended up loving the house and put an offer in the next day. Long story short, he ended up buying the house.

CHAPTER 6

FINANCING YOUR HOME

Buying a home as a physician gives you lots of great options. You can use a traditional loan with a 20 percent down payment or you can use other loan products, such as physician loans or other lower down payment loan products. The advantage of a physician loan is that you have more wiggle room on your debt to income ratio in regards to your student loan debt. There are other loan programs that are available to physicians that don't require a MD or DO. These programs may allow as little as 5 to 10 percent down, depending on the cost of the house. There are even some zero-down home loan programs. No matter what type of home loan program you choose to go with, it's important to have the best credit score possible so you can receive the lowest interest rate.

When you are in escrow, you should have loan applications with at least three different lenders. I suggest you have a mortgage application with your bank, a good physician loan program, and a mortgage broker. This allows you to have peace of mind that if one application falls through, you have other options. Trust me when I say that something will go wrong at some point in your escrow. I'm not being negative; I'm just being realistic. Do not wait to the last minute to get your financing in order. This can lead to delays, expensive mistakes, or even worse, the loss of your loan. Having multiple applications also allows for bargaining power on the interest rate. A difference of 0.1 percent can lead to thousands to tens of thousands of dollars of savings over the life of a loan, depending on the purchase price.

Once you start your loan application process, you lock in your rate. This means that you need to know what the going rate for a mortgage is. Mortgage rates change daily, so keep an eye on the market. Also, you can negotiate with the banks to lower your interest rate to be competitive. Make sure to lock in your rate with a time frame that is longer than the length of your escrow. Sometimes escrow can take longer than expected. For example, if you have a 21-day escrow, you should lock in your rate for at least 30 days or even more. This gives you peace of mind. Make sure to ask what happens if your escrow takes longer than expected and get the answer you received in writing.

As mentioned earlier, your credit score plays a huge role in what loan products you qualify for.

You should have started building and increasing your credit long before trying to buy a house. The higher your credit score, the better the interest rate you will have, and the more money you will save over the life of the loan. The best way to build your credit is to pay all your bills on time and not max out your credit cards. The higher the available credit you a have on your credit cards, the better your credit score will be.

CHAPTER 7

PUTTING IN AN OFFER

Once you have found a house you love, you will need to submit an offer and either a pre-qualification letter or pre-approval letter. A pre-qualification letter states how much a bank will probably loan you. The bank does a quick look at your finances and gives you an estimate on how much house you can buy. A pre-approval from the bank takes a much deeper look at your finances. The bank will look at things like your employment history, income, debt, credit scores, and tax returns to determine the maximum amount you can borrow and the interest rate you will receive. As you can imagine, submitting a pre-approval letter with your offer carries more weight than a pre-qualification letter.

There are several strategies to getting your offer accepted on the house of your dreams. If the seller is a family or individual, you or your real estate agent should write a letter to them stating why you love the house. Talk about the things you like about the house and what you would cherish and never change. Give them basic details about yourself, such as where you grew up, where you went to school, and how many children you have. Do not talk about what you would change or don't like about the house. Many people have had their offer accepted because of the letter they wrote to the seller. Remember, a seller can sell their house to whomever they please. If the seller likes you, they will accept your offer.

If the seller is an investor, pulling on heartstrings will probably not work. Many investors use hard money loans to flip houses. Hard money loans are loans to investors based on the value of the property and have a very high interest rate. This makes the investor very motivated to sell the house as fast as possible for as much as possible. The best strategy when dealing with investors is to be a strong candidate. That means putting 20 percent down and having good financial reserves. This decreases the chance of having any problems with your loan.

Regardless of if the seller is an individual, family, or investor, it is important to make a fair offer. Do not lowball them. It will create a bad impression, and they will not take your offer seriously. Make a fair offer from the beginning. How do you know how much to offer? Your real estate agent is an expert in knowing what to offer. This is done by looking at comparables or "comps" in your neighborhood. This is the amount for which homes similar to the one you are buying were sold. This information is also used by the banks for appraising the value of your house.

It is very common to receive a counter-offer after submitting your initial offer, especially if you are trying to buy a house in a desirable area. The seller will often ask for your best and final offer. This may lead to a bidding war behind the scenes. Sometimes it's a ploy to get more money out of you. No matter what, do not submit an offer you cannot afford to pay or an amount that you are unhappy with. Do not submit an offer on a house that you are not excited about. If your offer is accepted, you want to be happy and ready to move forward. At the same time, you must be willing to walk away at any point in time before the close of escrow if things are not working out for you. Remember, a home is one of the most expensive purchases you will make in your lifetime, and you need to be happy with it.

CHAPTER 8

OFFER ACCEPTED! NOW WHAT?

Now that your offer has been accepted, the real fun begins. The home-buying process can be surprisingly emotional. Get ready to experience all kinds of emotions. You will sign a purchase agreement, and you will need to give an earnest money deposit (aka good faith deposit), which is usually 3 percent of the purchase price of the house. Escrow fees will be charged. The purchase agreement will state who pays for the escrow fees. This is negotiable, and you should consult your real estate agent regarding this. You will also get a list of disclosures about the house and will need to sign a contract detailing what needs to be done in order to close escrow, or buy the house.

There will be a list of contingencies or conditions that need to be met in order to move forward to buy the house. Common ones are the inspection, appraisal, and finance contingencies. For example, an inspection needs to be done within 14 days of escrow, and it needs to be to the buyer's liking in order to close escrow. While the contingencies are negotiable, you should definitely have contingencies for finance, appraisal, and inspection as a first-time homebuyer.

The inspection is of the utmost importance. It will allow you see exactly what is wrong with the house. The buyer pays for the inspection. The cost depends on where you live and the square footage of the house. It is nonrefundable. Your real estate agent should be able to recommend a good inspection company to you. Your real estate agent should definitely be present for the inspection. If possible, you should also be there. You should get a general inspection and specialized inspections as needed. For example, if you live on a hill, you should have an inspection that specializes on the home's foundation. If the home was previously in escrow, you can ask to see previous inspection reports. Once you have the inspection, you can negotiate with the buyer on what should and shouldn't be fixed by the close of escrow.

In order to get a loan, your bank will require an appraisal. The buyer is usually expected to pay for this too. The appraiser will look at homes that are similar to yours that have sold within the last year or so to determine how much your potential home is worth. If the appraisal comes in at your offer price or higher, everything is good. However, if the appraisal comes back lower than your offer price, you have two options. You can either pay the difference or negotiate a lower price with the seller. The bank will not give you a loan for more than what the house has been appraised for. This serves to protect both the financial interest of the bank and the buyer.

To summarize, as the buyer, you will be expected to give an earnest money deposit of typically 3 percent of the purchase price to the escrow company. You will also be expected to pay for any necessary home inspections and appraisal fees. The appraised value of the house will be used by the bank to determine the amount they will lend you. Later on, you will be paying closing costs, which will be in addition to your down payment.

CHAPTER 9

ESCROW

An escrow company is a neutral third party that helps with several things, including holding the earnest money funds, keeping track of legal documents, and making sure all the conditions of the sale are met prior to closing. The escrow company also works with your loan officer to facilitate the loan process and the release of funds. They do not negotiate anything. They also cannot give you any legal or tax advice.

A title company conducts a title search and issues title insurance. In some states, the title company and the escrow companies are the same entity. In other states or counties, the title and escrow company are separate and will be charging separate fees. The title search will look for any liens or judgments made against the property. It will also look for any unpaid taxes on the property amongst other things. As you can imagine, this search is extremely important. Basically, the title company looks for anything that can hinder the sale of the property. Once it is determined that the title is clear, title insurance will be issued. This protects the buyer from fraudulent owner claims down the line. Oftentimes, the seller pays for the title insurance. This, too, is negotiable, and you need to read your purchase agreement.

Lenders also require the property to have title insurance. Rules for title companies vary state to state. That means that the cost of title insurance may also vary state to state. It is important to know the law for your state. This is where your trusty real estate agent comes into play. He or she should be able to answer your specific questions or at least be able to refer you to someone who can.

Due diligence is extremely important when buying a house. There are many people involved in the process. You, as a buyer, need to be knowledgeable about all the steps of closing. The lender and escrow company work closely together. Whenever a document or information is requested from you, make sure you give it to them in a timely manner. There are deadlines, and many different people have to review and approve everything. It also helps to regularly check in with the escrow company. They can alert you to any possible problems or delays.

A very common cause for delays is the bank. Yes, I just blamed someone. It's the truth. Financing is one of the most tedious parts of buying a home. That's why it is absolutely necessary to have a reliable, diligent, and truthful loan officer or broker.

Remember, you are dealing with hundreds of thousands of dollars, maybe even millions of dollars. This brings us to underwriting, which is detailed in the next chapter.

CHAPTER 10

THE UNDERWRITING PROCESS

The underwriting process is used to determine your eligibility for a home loan. You must meet all the qualifications for your loan, which varies by loan product. For example, if you are applying for a physician loan, you will have to show proof that you are a practicing physician. The bank will often ask for a copy of your medical degree, state medical license, and employment contract.

The underwriter's job is to verify every single piece of information you give. That means you will be bombarded with phone calls and emails about documentation. It is not uncommon to provide information like your last paycheck stub, only to be asked for that same exact piece of information a few weeks later. Do not complain or question them. This only leads to delays and prolongs your escrow. Give them the information again and keep a copy of it just in case you have to resubmit it.

During the underwriting process, the lender will take an in-depth look at your finances. They will look at information such as your past bank statements, your income, your student loan debt, your credit history, and your monthly purchases. One important component is your debt to income ratio. This is the ratio of how much you spend a month on bills (e.g. rent, car note, credit cards) to how much money you make in a month. It ideally needs to be less than 38 percent. There is some wiggle room with that. The advantage of a physician loan is that they don't hold your student loans against you as much as they do with a traditional loan. The bank realizes that as a doctor, you have high earning potential. They also know that doctors are less likely to default on their loans, and if the going gets tough, you will be able to increase your income by taking more calls or seeing more patients.

Please understand that you are under a microscope during the underwriting process. They will be looking at every single purchase you make. They will also be keeping a close eye on how much money is deposited into your bank accounts. This is not the time to make any big purchases or change your spending and savings habits. That is why you need to prepare months in advance to buy a house. It's also why you should have a strict budget that you follow. I have heard many horror stories about how everything was fine until an excited buyer bought an appliance for their new house and ended up disqualifying themselves from their loan.

This is not the time to open new lines of credit either. Every time you apply for a new line of credit, an inquiry is made on your credit report. Having too many inquiries on your credit sends a red flag to the lender. They will ask you to explain it. They will also look at your rental history and may even contact your landlord to make sure you live where you say you live and that you pay your rent on time. Be ready to explain everything verbally and then write an email stating what you said as written proof. The underwriting process is serious business.

CHAPTER 11

CLOSING THE DEAL

Closing on your home is an invigorating and scary process. Now that all the stars and moons have aligned, you can do your final walk-through before settlement. This means that all the contingencies have been met, your lender has verified everything and has approved your loan, you have lined up a home insurance company, and the title has been cleared. The final walk-through should not be done last minute. This step is extremely important. It should be done a couple of days before closing day. I recommend that both the buyer's and seller's real estate agents be there.

The final walk-through allows you the see the house one more time and make sure that any repairs that have been agreed upon have been done. I recommend that you not only verify with your own eyes that the repairs have been done, but also get a copy of the receipts for them. The house should be delivered clean and empty. If it is not, the seller should arrange to have it cleaned. They can either hire someone to clean the house or give you the money to have someone do it.

Once you are happy with the final walk-through, you will sign all the closing documents and pay the closing costs, and the loan will be funded. Funds are usually given via wire transfer or cashier's check.

The closing costs at this point will be a good-faith estimate of all of the costs. This means that the actual closing costs may be a little higher or lower. The escrow company tends to overestimate the cost so you can receive a small refund after closing versus owing even more money. You will need to sign your closing documents with a notary public. Make sure that everything on the paperwork matches up, such as names, the purchase price, and the interest rate of the loan. If you have any questions, make sure they are answered to your complete satisfaction before signing anything. For example, verify that there is no penalty for paying off your home loan early. Also, in all of the excitement, remember to bring personal identification. Forgetting to do so is a very common mistake that is made.

Once your loan has been funded, the house is now yours. Congratulations! The closing costs include the first year of homeowner's insurance and taxes. Expect a supplementary tax bill in a few months. It will reflect the new tax amount owed on the property. The closing cost also includes your first mortgage payment. The mortgage payment includes principle and interest payments of the loan. After closing, your next mortgage payment is due one full month after the last day of the month of your closing. This differs from rent, which is paid a month in advance.

It is worth noting that when you pay anything above your monthly mortgage payment, that amount will be applied to the principal balance of the loan. This will not only help you pay off the loan faster, but will also decrease the amount of interest you will pay, thus saving you money. Making one extra mortgage payment a year can make a huge difference and shaves off several years from your mortgage. One way to do this is by paying half of your mortgage every two weeks. Since there are 52 weeks in a year, you will make 26 half-payments a year. Therefore, you will make 13 full payments in one year. It is a simple and pain-free way to make one extra mortgage payment a year.

ACKNOWLEDGMENTS

I would like to thank all the people who have motivated me to pursue my dream of medicine and entrepreneurship. All my life, I have wanted to become a physician. My primary goal was to get into medical school, survive residency, and become a doctor. Before I knew it, the time had passed, and I was an attending physician. While I enjoyed medicine and helping people, I felt like something was missing. I realized that I wanted to become an entrepreneur as well. Shortly afterwards, I bought my first house. I discovered an unexpected passion for real estate. I decided to combine medicine and real estate by helping doctors navigate the home-buying process. I would like to thank my grandfather, Cleveland Alexander Winge, for believing in me since the moment I said I wanted to be a doctor. I would also like to thank my parents, Dr. Ralph Winge and Mrs. Lydia Cooper-Winge, for supporting me every step of the way, and my cousin, Adam

Winge, for his helpful advice. Also, I give a warm thank you to my business coach, Dr. Draion Burch. Last but not least, I would like to thank James Blake Wilson Jr. for being my biggest cheerleader and nurturer. I could not have written this book without him.

SOCIAL MEDIA

Website:
www.drgoldie.com

LinkedIn:
www.linkedin.com/in/drgoldiemd

Facebook:
www.facebook.com/drgoldiemd

Instagram:
@drgoldiemd

Twitter:
@drgoldiemd

Pinterest:
@drgoldiemd

Schedule a complimentary
15-minute strategy session:
www.drgoldiemd.com

ABOUT THE AUTHOR

Dr. Goldie Winge is a board-certified anesthesiologist born and raised in Los Angeles, California. She received her Bachelor of Science in Psychobiology from the University of California, Riverside, and her medical degree from the UCLA/Drew Medical Education Program. Afterwards, she completed her anesthesiology training at Beth Israel Deaconess Medical Center, a Harvard Medical School-affiliated teaching hospital in Boston, Massachusetts.

In addition to medicine, Dr. Winge is also passionate about real estate and has authored two e-books on the industry: *12 Steps to Paying for Your Home* and *How to Save $5000 on Contractors*. Dr.

Winge also loves teaching, traveling, writing, and connecting people to the right opportunities. She currently lives in Los Angeles with her partner, James Blake Wilson Jr., and their dog, Riley.

To connect, visit her website at
www.drgoldie.com

CREATING DISTINCTIVE BOOKS
WITH INTENTIONAL RESULTS

We're a collaborative group of creative masterminds with a mission to produce high-quality books to position you for monumental success in the marketplace.

Our professional team of writers, editors, designers, and marketing strategists work closely together to ensure that every detail of your book is a clear representation of the message in your writing.

Want to know more?
Write to us at info@publishyourgift.com
or call (888) 949-6228

Discover great books, exclusive offers, and more at
www.PublishYourGift.com

Connect with us on social media

@publishyourgift

www.ingramcontent.com/pod-product-compliance
Lightning Source LLC
Chambersburg PA
CBHW041959080526
44588CB00021B/2800